10-Minute Crafts

CHRISTMAS CRAFTS

ANNALEES LIM

WINDMILL
BOOKS
New York

Published in 2016 by Windmill Books,
an Imprint of Rosen Publishing
29 East 21st Street, New York, NY 10010

Editor: Elizabeth Brent
Craft stylist: Annalees Lim
Designer: Dynamo Ltd
Photographer: Simon Pask, NI Studios

Picture acknowledgements:
All step-by-step craft photography: Simon Pask,
NI Studios; images used throughout for creative
graphics: Shutterstock

Cataloging-in-Publication Data

Lim, Annalees.
Christmas crafts / by Annalees Lim.
p. cm. — (10-minute crafts)
Includes index.
ISBN 978-1-5081-9077-6 (pbk.)
ISBN 978-1-5081-9078-3 (6-pack)
ISBN 978-1-5081-9079-0 (library binding)
1. Christmas decorations — Juvenile literature.
2. Handicraft — Juvenile literature. I. Lim,
Annalees. II. Title.
TT900.C4 L56 2016
745.594'12—d23

Manufactured in the United States of America
CPSIA Compliance Information: Batch #BW16PK: For Further Information contact
Rosen Publishing, New York, New York at 1-800-237-9932

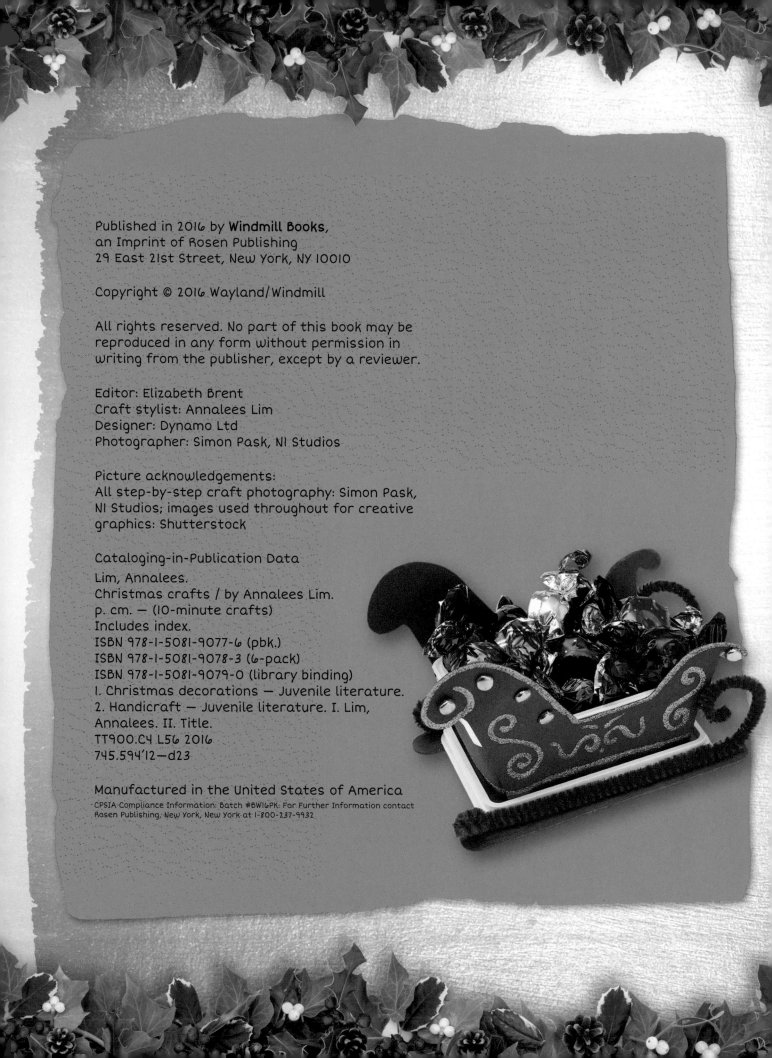

Contents

Christmas

There is no better time to get crafty than at Christmas. You can use the projects in this book to make special, handmade gifts for your friends and family, or to create festive decorations. Each craft will take you only about 10 minutes, but don't feel the need to rush! You can build up some festive excitement by making and creating your way through December!

Elf: pages 14-15

Christmas is a great time to recycle, too. There will be lots of things that you might otherwise throw away that make great craft materials. Before you chuck it, check it! Can any packaging or boxes be flattened into pieces of card stock that you could use to make the stocking templates on pages 6-7? Is there any leftover Christmas wrapping paper that you can use to decorate the wreath on pages 10-11? Or can you save bits of ribbons from presents to make the elf's present on pages 14-15? There are lots more possibilities, so if you think something may be useful, save it and keep it in a safe place ready for the next time you get creative.

Crafting can be messy, especially if you are using glitter or glue, so make sure you cover all your work surfaces with old newspaper or a plastic tablecloth before you begin. Always wash your hands after you have used glue to keep your works of art from being ruined by sticky fingers, and always ask an adult to help you with scissors or sharp compasses.

Santa: pages 16-17

Robin: pages 22-23

So, put on a Christmas sweater and get messy!

A note about measurements

Measurements are given in U.S. form with metric in parentheses. The metric conversion is rounded to make it easier to measure.

Felt stocking

These mini stockings are perfect for storing tiny treats or candy canes. You could hang them on a Christmas tree or give them as a gift.

1 Draw a stocking shape that is no bigger than 6 x 6 inches (15 x 15 cm) onto some card stock, and cut it out to make a template.

2 Cut two stocking shapes out of the red felt, using the card stock template as a guide.

3 Sew some strips of ribbon onto one of the stocking shapes.

4 Place one of the stocking shapes on top of the other, with the decoration facing outwards, and sew around the outside, leaving the top open.

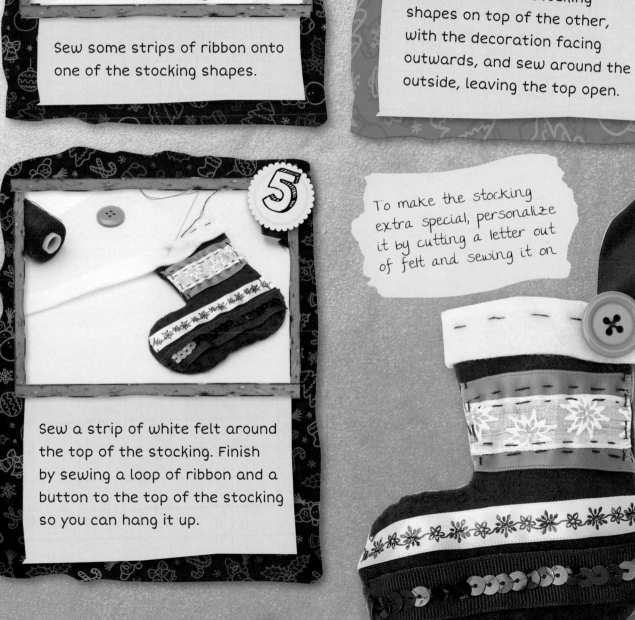

5 Sew a strip of white felt around the top of the stocking. Finish by sewing a loop of ribbon and a button to the top of the stocking so you can hang it up.

To make the stocking extra special, personalize it by cutting a letter out of felt and sewing it on

Sleigh candy dish

Dashing through the snow can be hungry work! Use this handy dish to serve up some Christmas treats.

1

Draw two sleigh shapes onto some red card stock, making sure they are big enough to cover the long sides of your container.

2

Cut them out and stick them onto the container using sticky pads.

3

Cut some more card stock to cover the front and back of the container and attach it using sticky pads.

4

Stick the sleigh onto the lid with sticky pads, then stick all of this onto the two Popsicle sticks, using more sticky pads. Curl up some pipe cleaners to make the skis, and glue them onto the sticks.

5

Decorate the sides with paper fasteners and swirls of glitter glue and leave to dry completely before filling with candy.

Make nine of the reindeer on pages 12-13 and attach them to the sleigh using some sparkly string

Paper ribbon wreath

Display your cards in this pretty indoor wreath made from paper and cardboard.

You will need:

- A pair of compasses
- A ruler
- A pencil
- Corrugated cardboard
- Scissors
- String
- Craft glue
- Assorted green paper
- A glue stick
- Red tissue paper

1

Use your compasses to draw a 12-inch (30 cm) circle with a 6-inch (15 cm) circle inside it onto the corrugated cardboard to make a ring. Repeat, so you have two rings in total, and then cut both out.

2

Use the compasses to make a small hole at the top of one of the rings. Tie some string through this hole to make a loop.

3

Spread glue over one of the rings. Stick the two rings together, leaving the knot on the string on the outside.

4

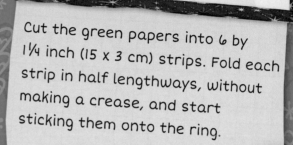

Cut the green papers into 6 by 1¼ inch (15 x 3 cm) strips. Fold each strip in half lengthways, without making a crease, and start sticking them onto the ring.

5

Rip the tissue paper into small pieces and roll these into balls. Glue the balls around the ring in clusters of three.

Change the green paper for strips of leftover wrapping paper to make your own wreath.

Toilet paper tube reindeer

No Christmas scene is complete without a reindeer or two. You could even try making all nine of Santa's reindeer: Dasher, Dancer, Prancer, Vixen, Comet, Cupid, Donner, Blitzen, and, of course, Rudolph!

You will need:

- Two toilet paper tubes
- Brown paper
- Scissors
- A glue stick
- Brown pipe cleaners
- Adhesive tape
- A stapler
- Craft glue
- Googly eyes
- White paper
- A brown bead

1

Cut some brown paper to fit around the tubes, and glue it in place.

2

Place two pipe cleaners inside one of the tubes and fix in place with sticky tape. Bend them to make legs, then bend up the ends to make feet so the reindeer can stand.

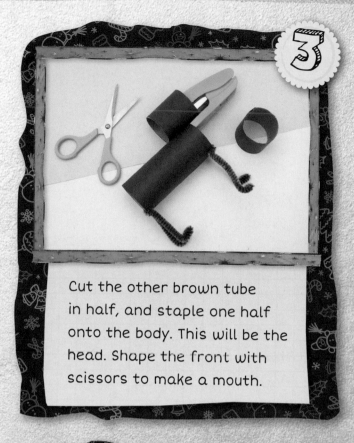

3

Cut the other brown tube in half, and staple one half onto the body. This will be the head. Shape the front with scissors to make a mouth.

4

Staple another two pipe cleaners to the top of the head and bend them into antler shapes.

5

Glue some googly eyes onto the face and make a tail from brown and white scrap paper. Glue a brown bead to the top of the head to make a nose.

Decorate the Christmas dinner table with a reindeer in each place, and write each person's name on the side to make seasonal place settings.

Pinecone elf

Getting some fresh air at Christmas can be fun after all that food! Next time you're out and about, try collecting some pinecones so you can make a team of Christmas elves to help Santa out!

1

Use the fabric glue to stick the flesh-colored pom-pom to the top of the pinecone. Stick the two googly eyes onto the pom-pom.

2

Wrap one pipe cleaner around the top of the pineone to make the arms and the other pipe cleaner around the bottom to make the legs. Bend up the bottom of the legs to make feet and make sure the elf can stand up straight.

14

3

Cut out a semicircle of green felt 2 inches (5 cm) in diameter. Fold this into a cone shape and stick the edges together using fabric glue. Glue the small white pom-pom on the point and stick the hat to the head.

4

Cut out four mitten shapes from the red felt. Glue two mitten shapes to the end of each arm, sandwiching the pipe cleaners.

Remember to always wash your winter finds before you start using them to make elves. When you are out, you may also find acorns and shells. These are great to make mini elves with!

5

Decorate your elf with a red felt stripe around the hat, and a red zigzag collar around the neck. You could also make a felt present with a red ribbon for the elf to hold in its arms.

Santa tree decoration

This jolly Santa will Ho-Ho-Ho-pefully add some Christmas cheer to the top of your tree.

You will need:

- Scissors
- Red card stock
- A paper doily
- White paper
- Flesh-colored paper
- A glue stick
- Green card stock
- A black marker
- A stapler
- Fabric glue
- A small, white pom-pom

1

Cut out a circle of red card stock that is slightly smaller than the paper doily. Cut the doily and the card stock in half so you have four semicircles. You will only need one semicircle of card stock and one semicircle of doily to make a Santa. Save the other halves to make another one later.

2

Cut out a beard and mustache from white paper and a face shape from flesh-colored paper. Stick them together with the glue stick. Cut some red arms and green mittens out of card stock, and stick them together, too.

Draw around the face and arms with the marker pen.

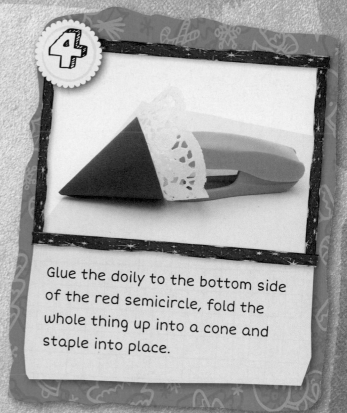

Glue the doily to the bottom side of the red semicircle, fold the whole thing up into a cone and staple into place.

Stick the face and arms onto the cone, and glue the white pom-pom to the top.

Make lots of Santas and fasten them together in a long line to make a Christmas decoration that you can hang from the ceiling or along a wall.

Candy cane Christmas card

Everyone loves receiving a Christmas card, but this card is also a gift! Secretly store a delicious candy cane inside to send a little treat to someone special.

1

Fold your white card stock in half and make a firm crease.

2

With the card still folded, cut a 3/8-inch (1 cm) slit in the fold that is 3/4 inch (2 cm) from the bottom, and another one 2 inches (5 cm) to the right of it.

3

Open the card up and press the cut pieces inwards to make a long box shape. Be sure to press down firmly to make a good crease.

4

Turn the card upside down, and hook the curved part of the candy cane into the box. Secure it in place with sticky tape.

5

Turn the card the right side up, and transform the candy cane into a Christmas tree by cutting out a yellow star for the top and a green tree shape to stick to the back of the cane. Use the stickers to decorate the rest of the card.

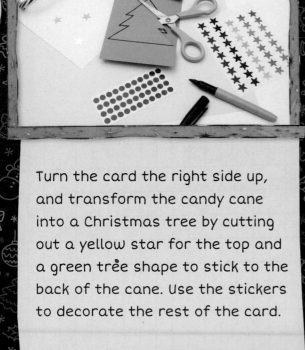

Your card could also be transformed into a North Pole scene. Stick an igloo shape behind the candy cane and draw some polar bears beside it.

Christmas tree advent calendar

The countdown to Christmas can begin with a homemade Advent calendar that you can personalize and decorate.

1

Cut the green card stock into a long triangle.

2

Starting ¾ inch (2 cm) from the bottom, draw and cut 12 slits, ¾ inch (2 cm) apart, on either side of the triangle, leaving a 5/8-inch (1.5 cm) gap between them in the middle.

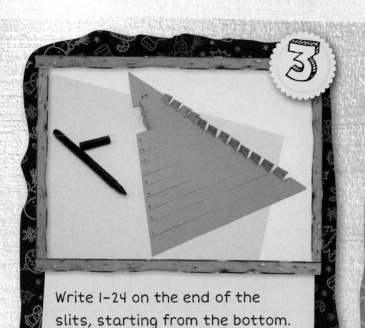

Write 1-24 on the end of the slits, starting from the bottom. Fold the end of each slit over by 5/8 inch (1.5 cm), leaving the bottom one unfolded. Write the matching number on the top of every flap.

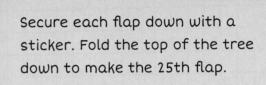

Secure each flap down with a sticker. Fold the top of the tree down to make the 25th flap.

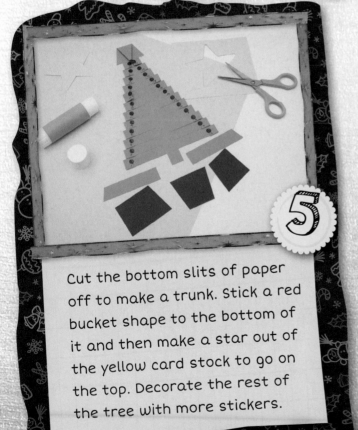

Cut the bottom slits of paper off to make a trunk. Stick a red bucket shape to the bottom of it and then make a star out of the yellow card stock to go on the top. Decorate the rest of the tree with more stickers.

You don't just have to make a Christmas tree shape - try cutting slits up the sides of a present shape, a star, or even a round ornament.

Rocking robin ornament

Turn a plain ornament into a fun, quirky character that will brighten up any Christmas tree.

1

Cut out felt shapes to decorate your ornament. You will need two brown wings, a yellow beak made from two triangles, and a red circle.

2

Use the fabric glue to stick all the felt shapes to the ornament.

3

Add a googly eye to each side of the ornament, sticking them in place using the fabric glue.

4

Bend a pipe cleaner into claw shapes and glue them to the bottom of the ornament.

Try decorating a silver bulb to look like a Christmas pudding, complete with felt holly leaves on top!

5

Add some sparkle by decorating the felt with glitter glue.

Websites

For web resources related to the subject of this book, go to:
www.windmillbooks.com/weblinks and select this book's title.

Glossary

antlers solid, bony growths on the head of a deer

doily a small napkin made of lace or lace-like paper

festive about a festival or a holiday

igloo a dome-shaped house made of blocks of ice and snow

ornament a round, colored decoration hung on a Christmas tree

seasonal something that happens only at a certain time of year

wreath a ring-shaped decoration

Index